IN A RARE TIME OF RAIN

En Busca de mi Alma (Odalid, 1977)
The Confusion of Anglers (Wide Skirt Press, 1988)
Where Smoke Is (Wide Skirt Press, 1990)
Piltdown Man & Bat Woman (Spout Publications, 1994)

IN A RARE TIME OF RAIN

Milner Place

Chatto & Windus

LONDON

First published in Great Britain in 1995

1 3 5 7 9 10 8 6 4 2

Copyright © Milner Place 1995

Milner Place has asserted his right under the
Copyright, Designs and Patents Act, 1988 to be
identified as the author of this work

Acknowledgements are due to the editors of the following publications,
in which some of these poems first appeared:
*The Echo Room, joe soap's canoe, London Magazine, The North, Poetry
Wales, The Rialto, Scratch, Slow Dancer, Smith's Knoll, Spout, Sunk
Island Review, The Wide Skirt*

The poems 'Weather-wise', 'A Tight Ship' and 'Last Will and Testament'
were previously included in *Where Smoke Is* (Wide Skirt Press);
'The Log of the Sloop Exceed' was included in *The Confusion
of Anglers* (Wide Skirt Press)

Published in 1994 by
Chatto & Windus Limited
Random House, 20 Vauxhall Bridge Road
London SW1V 2SA

Random House Australia (Pty) Limited
20 Alfred Street, Milsons Point, Sydney
New South Wales 2061, Australia

Random House New Zealand Limited
18 Poland Road, Glenfield
Auckland 10, New Zealand

Random House South Africa (Pty) Limited
PO Box 337, Bergvlei, South Africa

Random House UK Limited Reg. No. 954009

A CIP catalogue record for this book is available from
the British Library

ISBN 0 7011 6251 1

Typeset by SX Composing Ltd, Rayleigh, Essex
Printed in Great Britain by
Mackays of Chatham PLC, Chatham, Kent

To Geoff Hattersley, Keith Jafrate,
David Morley, for faith and counsel.
To Dorothy for love.

*'I based my heart on this, I listened to all
the sorrowful salt'*
Pablo Neruda

Contents

THE PASSER-BY

He came to a valley where the choughs built nests
in the churches of failed gods, in a rare time of rain,
and stopped to smell the flowers that shivered like

a perfumed sea, rippling their pink and saffron blooms,
their velvet lips open to the sun dance of bees. If
there'd been any time to spare between his coming

and his going from this place, he would have stayed,
even gone back to fetch the one with auburn hair.
Four white stallions cantered across a plain so flat

the wind could get no purchase, blew wild with rage,
blew sounds so far and fast the drumming of the hooves
was never heard, the neighing lost, even to the third

generation. The riders in their sable cloaks drew tight
their lips, and clutched their voices in their cheeks;
rowelled their steeds' flanks with crimson spurs.

DARK WINGS

She thought this is my lucky day, when the *baas*
didn't beat her when she spilt the coffee, when
he didn't squeeze her young breasts and take her
like a sweating bull when the missie went shopping;

when she wasn't locked in the shed with no windows
for having forgotten to polish the horns of the kudu,
whose sad head hung over the mantelpiece gazing
at the twin tusks and assegais on the facing wall;

when they said she could go home for a night, even
to leave in the gold and pinks of the sunset, to walk
the dusty road through the wattle plantations, farms
where birds fluttered and dipped over the green corn.

The judge asked if she had anything to say. She said:
I saw the black widow-birds dancing in the mealie fields.

FAVELA

The sun hammers the corrugated iron,
cracks the thin boards; but over the sea
the clouds push their black hearts closer

and it is discussed that the evening
will be a washing out of the runnels of shit;
plastic buckets and old tins will find

their appropriate pitches, and the children
who go down to the city with boxes of brushes,
rags and polish, are near to becoming apathetic.
This afternoon the music is only anticipating
the drumbeat; aguardiente is opening the eyes
of old men and bright dresses are all the colours

of the desperation of hope. And this is a brief
time of the sleeping of spiders and a shining
of moonstones on the buckles of sad shoes.

ETUDE

Falling off the soft sound,
breaking the painted window to let in
the scent of gangrene; to see clearly
the toad writhing in a snake's gorge,

and the carnations
in the buttonholes of bankers.

And you should know
how Jose Cisneros died in the dark hut
to the clicking of rosaries;
lungs choked with broken rock
and no spare coins to close the eyes.

And I could tell you
how Felicidad Consuelo and Maria Benavides
were raped in the cells.
But you should know all this

from the cries of desolate birds,
muteness of dark-leafed trees.

A MOUNTAIN IN A BARE ROOM

The hard margins of cold panes compress
the silence; music is only smoke of woodwind,

drum of rain, and if you think you're dead
you're not far out. Today is mother's day,

the milk is on the doorstep, but in Peru
the earth shakes, mountains are on the move,

and in the Urals, bees compete with Geiger-counters.
Here between stolid walls, pursed lips,

the air is thicker than a huckster's skin, burning
the eyes that seek to see dust devils in a land

so far away, so dry and still that every sound
is made of glass.

LUM STREET

THERE WAS NEVER ANY KNOWING WITH
    SEPTIMUS ARKWRIGHT.

He was one of those who lived in a house without
    windows,
and although he wore thick-rimmed glasses, they only
    served

to reflect mist and coal-smoke that clung to his
    herringbone
overcoat, with its turned-up collar against August snow

or that type of rain that is the making of rainbows, and
in its other life causes night-lights to dance in northern
    skies,

and ecstasy in Pennine witches. If Arkwright was aware
of all this, he never let it affect the reasoning he wrapped

round his thin shoulders, until the day he discovered his
    wife
was not unfaithful with the milkman, but was doing a lot

of favours for a priest. And he didn't turn paler with rage,
but went straight to his friend who sold spurned books

in the market to buy a volume of Blake, and to a bucket
    shop
for a flight to Nepal. He is still there among mountains

and poppies, and he left his coat and spectacles in a room
without windows, with a bunch of white lilies for his wife.

THE WORST FEARS OF FISHFACE WAGSTAFF
ARE ABATED.

He didn't see Septimus Arkwright at first, partly
because he was at the other end of the bar, but more

for the reason that Arkwright, in his long herringbone
   coat,
resembled a false marble column, and was only identified

by a very slight motion. When Fishface finally separated
the coat from the column, he didn't stride across the room

to embrace and paw his friend, but dug his nose deeper
into his pint of very real ale, and tried to dream up

the colours of the winner of the Derby. And all this,
of course, was long before Septimus Arkwright took off

for Nepal, and was never seen in the Moulting Pigeon
   again.
But fate had it in for Fishface when war broke out

between two super soap salesmen, after an argument about
   Pliny
the Elder, and Septimus became a refugee in Wagstaff's

demilitarised zone. But today the sun shone in Lum Street,
all Wagstaff's fears proved rootless for Septimus never

mentioned the fiver, and Piggott won.

WAGSTAFF'S PASSION.

'Suspicion and insinuation are the water of life in Lum
Street, gossip its bread, and the trafficking of salacious
scandal a greasy spectre and anathema to appropriate
conclusions, and a constant source of social disorder. But
the fiercest wars, fought from doorstep to doorstep, corner
to corner, and even reaching beyond all natural frontiers,
into Neat Street and Butlin's Close, are over the nature of
the lights that shine in garrets and basements in those
hours when the clatter of beer cans dies away, and even
the cats call a truce.' A Chronicle of Woollaton,
Arthur Clutterbeck.
Grimesmere Press.

The stair creaked, the locks were opened, and he entered
the treasury. In the light of a candle, he carefully lifted
three glass-topped trays, and placed them on the table,

and only then
flooded the room with light.

And all the children of Albion sang.
And the heavens were opened and the forests bowed.

They were laid out in rows, wing to wing,
fritillary to fritillary, and all light
had come to their aid, to their stillness.
They were no deader
than a sun, no livelier
than a cold moon, and he
pulled up a chair, minutes
seeped out of their cracks,
and all the bitter juices
were drawn from his throat.

And when he left the room
down the well of the stairs,
he paused to listen
to the beating of wings,
and he smiled
his secret.

THE COURSE OF TRUE LOVE FOR MAVIS SHRIKE.

For fifteen identical years Coriolanus Brewster hung about
the sweet shop and tobacconist's Mavis Shrike had
    inherited
from her uncle, 'Calypso' Jones, who was divided by the
    third
to last tram to run down Lum Street. He wooed her gently

with overripe mangoes and sad lettuces that he earned
    from Ali
Asram, for bagging potatoes and unloading the
    remaindered
hearse that Ali used to fetch oranges and tomatoes from
    Osset.
But Cory never had the strength to speak of his love, even

though he had played Rugby League for Batley and
    Featherstone;
had fought Towzer Grimshaw for two quid at Dewsbury
    Fair. And
Mavis, though she smiled when he brought her rhubarb
    and figs,
was never bold enough to ask him how he liked his tea.

In her bedroom, hung with pietas and an outsized poster
of Johnny Weissmuller, she would rub her breasts when
    she saw
Coriolanus sweating as he pushed his barrow up the street;
bare-chested even on frosty mornings. They were married

in the church of Jude the Apostate by Wesley 'Grits'
    Mackay
before opening time on a Saturday, only five weeks after
Coriolanus had plucked his bride from a fire in her shop,
allegedly started by tinkers. But there were rumours.

NOSTRADAMUS CLARKE WAS BARRED FROM
    EVERY PUB

within a bookie's runner's round, except the Pigeon,
where the snug became his lair. His corner seat

was rarely cold from when Alf Hazeltwig slid out
all seven bolts to open up, until the end of time.

How he afforded all the stout, and when he ate, or if
he was circumcised were not the kind of questions asked

in Lum Street, except behind the thickest doors. He had
that kind of look, that kind of eye, by some accounts

an awesome knack with potter's clay, and read the entrails
of unfortunate pigs and sheep by moonlight in the abattoir

where Clifton Spratt was watchman. Furthermore his
    mother
kept a one-eyed cat and several warts beneath her chins.

But it was said, and rightly so, he knew a thing or two
about the pedigrees of dogs, and only lightly beat his Flo.

IDRIS BEN YUSEF

had flaming hair, lugubrious eyes, and played the basset-
    horn
on winter nights among the chippings of his joiner's shop;

believing the sawn properties of oak and walnut seize the
    notes
then throw them back smelling of sap and resonant as
    pine.

His feet brushed through curled shavings like a broken
    comb;
he smoked a water pipe and dreamt of whitewashed walls,
    hoopoes,

grey stallions, women at the well, blew out his heart, trilled
scales that hammered on the deal and shook the spiders
    couchant

on their webs. Some summer nights he and his clarinet
    were seen
and heard on Blackhope Moor, along Crow Edge to
    Falcondale.

CHRYSALIS JONES WASHED DOWN STEPS

at number ten – the 'castle' – between Bert Boddy's
betting shop and Amy Coldthwaite's Her'n Fringe.
Lamented Jones had been a brickie, knocked off
the roof to house his pigeon loft, built battlements
around and kept a catapult to hand for cats.

After the funeral, the widow Jones thought proper
to keep on his flock, and bought two jackdaws
from a half-travelling man, in memory, emblem
of her respect for all Lamented's years among
the restless broods; his peering at the sky
with fevered eyes, and praying home his birds.

Two weeks to the very day from the interment,
Chrysalis was sold a pair of golden orioles
by Nostradamus Clarke, and wasn't too far gone

in black before the Samson twins sussed out
a hidden passion, not yet flowered; brought her
two finches, a robin and a mistelthrush

they'd trapped in the bushes by Cod Beck. Lamented's
brother, Handy Taff, soon found himself three quarters
employed in the construction, from this and that,
of tenements to house magpies and tits, as Chrysalis
was battened on by anything that walked and had
a knack with gins and lime. Three kestrels

seven ducks, a one-eyed macaw, came as a job lot
from Rudolph Falk; the Samson twins chipped in again
with coots and waterhens from Mafeking Park,
until Lamented's castle roof was feathered
like an Ascot hat. Each autumn the unwary
southbound flocks were made to pay their toll;

the smaller parts of Lum Street scavenged for mice
and rats to pacify the owls and crows, and all
the widow's mites and florins went on provender.
Each spring the air was full of song, fluttering
of wings and piercing calls, soft cooing, and the sky
above wheeling with flights of amorous birds.

SAM LOWE AND BILLY BRIGHT WERE DROWNED

out by the Salvation Army band while
busking on the corner of Cork Lane;
wreaked their revenge on God
by defecating on holy ground
and pissing against church and
chapel doors, until good Father
Flynn stuck out his crook,
and booked them for his discos
in the crypt. They took to reverence
like fleas to dogs or priests to wine,

confessed like thrushes in the dawn,
showed Christian charity to all
except the members of the Sally Ann.

LUCRECE HEPMONDIKE WHO KEPT

the Welkom Kaff, was noted for her style of hair
that changed more often than traffic lights, and held
the record in Lum Street for breaking hearts of those
with an eye for apple tart and custard, hot scones

and buttered toast and beans, cream buns. She'd been
a dancer in a troupe and even stripped before the Queen
of Denmark in Neat Street was shut by order of the bench.
She played each suitor like a xylophone, rang all

the changes, plucked them like a harp, until their strings
were stretched to such extremes they lost their voices,
and could only croak their orders in her erotic ear.
She never left them off the hook; they sat around the Kaff

so many zombies in a catacomb.

CUTHBERT AND ARIADNE WEEKES WERE
  BARREN BUT

two boys in Butlin's Close had just his ears;
a girl in Neat Street just her hair. Her tongue

was livelier than a beached sprat on a trawler's deck,
his lips so close he warbled through his nose. He hunched

his shoulders when she spat her malice like a fireman's
hose. But every Mother's Day he bought her flowers,

his shirts were double ironed; when they went to Filey
for a week they rode the magic roundabouts, the dipper

hand in hand, and nestled on the pier. On bingo nights
in Weaver's Hall she called her card and his, in case

his mouth was frozen when their ship came in.

JEANIE MACPHERSON SHOULD HAVE SMELLED

like fish, considering, but behind her like a comet's wake
  she left
a bouquet blown about the street; and in the Moulting
  Pigeon it was

said they whiffed her essences before she reached the
  welcome mat.
Most days she worked to her elbows in scales and guts and
  tails;

slicing the pale flesh of cod and skate, pink salmon,
  mackerel, rainbow
trout. She floated in a marble sea among red snappers,
  anchovies and eels,

smoked herring and the like. Her legs, though much
  admired, seemed out
of place amidst a multitude of fins. A figure cut to draw
  the eye;

hair the colour of barley wine, a maraschino cherry mouth,
  skin soft
as yoghourt, lardy thighs, though some sniffed at her
  choice of scents.

THE DAY THAT OLLIE PETERSON SAW
GOD BEHIND

his allotment shed in Fowler's Bottom, became a wonder
to all those who raised thin carrots, leeks and slugs.
But Father Flynn was not amused and raised his sombre
  eyes
in question when he passed the holy spot. Ollie no longer

turned the sod, fondled pea pods and swedes, and grew
two inches at the very least. He talked in a higher pitch
and walked a slower step; he nodded like an earl to 'Grits'
Mackay, and on the hallowed day itself, poured the last
  drops

of Navy Rum onto Tom Grimeshaw's onion patch. He
  swore
that God had beetroot hair, beard wrapped round his
  shoulders
as a scarf, flat cap and told him confidentially he was gob-
smacked at all this weeding out of what he'd meant should
  grow

in this here spot. That was the day that Ollie downed his
  hoe,
locked up his shed, but didn't leave his lot; now spends
long hours in vigilance, among his nettles, worts and
  docks.

ELIZA AND HAMLET BUCKLEJOHN WERE
RARELY SEEN

in daylight hours; not very noticeable at night.
Their room over the dead bakery, become O'Reilly's

Video Store, was curtained with white sheets so
thin that with a bulb of only 40 watts they lived

their public life as silhouettes. They kept the pale
secrets of their lives as close as teddy bears,

and drifted the dark streets, two purring cats. He had
a pony tale and she a bun, and both as thin as cabbage

soup, so that their faces shone with feverish eyes.
At night they danced in the spare room, two marionettes,

black on white.

THE THUNDER OF GOD'S VOICE WOKE

Franklin Armathwaite each Sunday from unholy dreams
of Jenny Pitt, through the fierce mouth of Abraham

Pocklington, a preacher in the Church of Hope, who had
a detailed knowledge of his master's will and all

the complex goings-on in Heaven, and most particularly
the other spot. But Franklin never held a grudge for long;

the voices warned him when to rise, put on his only suit
and socks, bow tie, and step out for a happy hour.

BARNADO STOAT, A CORNET IN THE
    TUNGSTONE MILL

& Hawthorn Foundry Band, and potman in the Pigeon,
slipped behind the bar at every chance to feed
the tape deck with marches, fifes and drums enough
to raise a sergeant major from the dead. He'd wink

at Lucius Snape, who soloed on the flute, stood in
for Arnold Batley, piccolo, whenever he'd his turns.

Barnado had a banshee's laugh that frightened widows
from their weeds, and Amos the ragman's donkey

on its rounds to such effect his master fitted out
the ass's ears with plugs, hobbled it well up the street
when calling for his mild and stout. On May Day the band
turned out in strength and threadbare uniforms to sweep

the cobwebs from the street, and taunt the Blue Boys
from Duck Lane, until they left to blow their bubbles
in another place. Next morning the startled paperboys,
the waking birds, were greeted with the Skater's Waltz.

THE WASTELAND BESIDE COD BECK ABOVE

the run-off from the abattoir, on summer nights
was loud with thumping, grunts and gasps, and half
the first-born of Lum Street were got among
the bushes and wrecked cars, despite more rubber
than a year's production on a Malay plantation.
There Amy Prout was fertilised by Herbert Dance,
and Phyllis Bundle well and truly laid by Elvis
Cockermouth. Even the quietest girls it seemed went
wild among the empty cans and nettle beds, and Lum
Street could be said to owe heart, soul and breath
to those brief humpings on the abandoned plot.

A POSTCARD OF WHITE MOUNTAINS

did the rounds with Alvin Potts, the postman, revealing
it to everyone before it came to rest with writs
and final notices on Fishface Wagstaff's mat.

A yak, a pretty dark-eyed girl, some doves, a Buddhist
monastery stigmatised with a rough cross, to mark the spot
where Arkwright laid his head and dreamed his
    confidential

and erotic paragraphs. *They keep a lot of bees, the Summer's*
hot. The Spring gets warmer but the Autumn frosts. The girls
are friendly but some monks are not. Last month it snowed

and snowed and iced, so that I fell and broke my opium pipe.
Last week it hailed. Today it's raining like a parson's mouth.
Wish you were here. Keep smiling. Yours, Sep. Ark.

RENDEZVOUS

You come when the leaves are stiff with frost. We drink
the juices of dark grapes, in which the sun has slept
through seasons of arrogance and the usual wars,
chimes of monumental clocks, cold mist of prayers
in icy cloisters, rise and fall of tides.

It shall be drunk, this wine, its sweet and bitter breath,
leaving a purple stain until the rain washes the glass
as clean as bones whitening in heather; clear as the music
of a blue wind, bright as a marble tomb in dew, sharp
as a shepherd's knife, smooth as panthers' claws.

The conversation drifts between the candles, slow-burning
to their night. Time changes clothes and colours, runs
from the bottle neck from dark to lighter red. You seem
to say so much, but all I hear are mercenary winds
scattering the sunburnt leaves among gnarled vines.

CIRCE

When the first martin settled in the eaves she took
her broom and swept the parlour clean, invited

in the morning, out the winter spiders, hung cloves
of garlic at the gate, rubbed her breasts with oil

of lavender, her thighs with musk, and waited
for the gorse to bloom. He came, playing a cornet,

singing of Nellie Dean, rapped with hard knuckles
on her door. And all the summer curlews called at night,

the stream that muttered by was spawned with silver
bream; until the wheat was raped, the red-apple-fall,

the martins and the singing pig went south.

THE WATCHMAN

All the sky was cold marble,
slivers fell into the streets
with the sound of amazed daggers,
and in his room he looked down

and noticed how the veins
on the back of his hands stood out,
the dryness of the skin. But he felt
young because it was a time of dancing.

He began to sway to the music
of the cold and the grey light, held
in his arms the soft flesh
of his remembering, breathed in

the scent of talc, and fresh-
washed hair, and the perfume
that is left on the wind
by songs of gypsies. And the same night,

in the warehouse, when the moon
dropped through the skylights,
when the long hours stretched
and the cats sampled the rough sacking

with curved claws, he danced again,
with feet so light the dust
slept on the concrete, danced
to the winged laughter of moths.

DOORSTEPS

Some nights are full
of questions, and the forgotten
open unpainted doors. You ask:
How was the flight? Did you
travel well, was the accommodation
up to scratch? The sea warm
and did you try that wine?

Some greet you
in grave tones, some laugh, embrace,
invite you in, but many
slam the door, tell you
to bugger off, respect
their privacy, and you become
more nervous with each knock.

ALL CHANGE

I took off my hat
to the station-master. He
responded: 'The slow engine

of pale days is scarcely heard,
there is little of significance.
But there are cracks

in the planed timbering;
there the light is fiercer,
the eye drawn like a bee,

green hills wash into greener
seas, the clock replaced
and there are many meetings,

much smoke and brandy, fresh
christened sheets and all
those voices, faces,

slow and piteous ships, rough
lodgings; lost eyes are met
again, become as content, warm

as bedroom slippers, and those
who died behind your back
make their apologies.'

TOP HOLD

He stopped on the shoulder
of the mountain. Looked back.

The land fell away, poured away
into the west and, below the wings
of scavengers, the smoke of scant fires
that warmed the messes of potatoes,

beans and scraps of lard, had no authority.
He recalled the warmth of eyes in doorways,
smooth hardened mud floors where everywhere
the earth battled with the relentless

tumbling of water and rock; children
clung to bent backs, men and women
looked down over the stunted trees
with scorn for eaters of rice and fish.

The deep valleys ran down as best they could, gathering
in their armpits the excrement of mountains and planting
gardens a little green, some emerald and olive beside
the hasty water; some flowers for the braver bees, berries

for orioles, and there were voles that contented grey foxes.
Here the people were divided, some playing harps,
some flutes;
fear ran uphill and envy looked down through the mists
and inferior clouds, onto roads and buildings of stone.
These men

hadn't the eyes of hawks and the women were
forever glancing
sideways; the valleys penned them tight despite
the invention
of radios, but they had no clocks, and they danced in
the most
propitious seasons for the god of thorns, and great birds.

Beyond, although the cities
were old in the eyes of men,
their generations were not
really that numerous.

They had a variety
of tombs, offices,
and cathedrals; the land
was fleeced of trees; so

that there was no
holding the rain for any
length of time, and what
had been a joy

to termites had become
the refuge of snakes
and lizards that knew
all the arts of patience.

The humans were vigorous
in digging pits, darting
and scurrying, but
their bellies

had become ulcerated,
their voices cracked
and they were addicted
to civilisation.

Beyond the nearest cities the deserts
clutched in their silences the bones
of the kings and emperors who had been
careless enough to omit names and titles

on their mausoleums, and the streets
and temples of their capitals. Even
their gods had been desiccated by the harsh
winds, shrunken into potbellied figurines

no larger than bulls' testicles, and cast out
to lie among great heaps of the disembowelled
shells of oysters, clams, and conches
that were the citadels of scorpions.

The ocean was little changed. It stretched and stretched;
it rolled and rolled and like a whale oblivious to sea-lice

and barnacles, ignored the self-important wriggling of ships
in their transportations of fruits and armories, slaves

and quartermasters, fish meal and the harvests of bankers;
of merchants and their mistresses, ship's orchestras

playing to the dancers of dreams giftwrapped in tinsel
by advertisers and newspaper proprietors. Ports painted

estuaries with oil, the sky with pink and orange vapours,
the pastel mud with the bodies of starved children.
Sawmills

shrieked and the ears of the wives of politicians
were muffled by furs of minks and chinchillas. Fishermen

fished. Priests consoled their widows and shipowners
with a heaven whose god started life as a carpenter, rose

to become the director of great corporations; they listened
covetously to the slavering confessions of rapists.

So he turned to the north,
shielding his eyes from the glare of ice.

There the hard face of the mountain
neither frowned nor smiled, but shone
with diamond eyes; and the wind

that trailed streamers of snow sang
with the voices of wolves. Behind

the mountain

a mountain   a mountain   a mountain

a mountain   a mountain

and the mountains

in their shakos and busbies marched into a sky as blue,
as grey, as black as the sea. The regiments crossed
the belt of the world, up to the neck of the land
where oceans shouted to each other across a
throat bedecked
with emeralds, a stole woven from green
mosses embroidered
with silk butterflies dyed in the colours of raindrops,

and there were sorrowful pelicans.

He heard all the voices
of the fires, saw
into the white heat
with its terrible rage;

into the labyrinths,
veins, arteries
of rock, into
the rising lust.

How the fire spewed
rubies, lapis lazuli;
reached up with golden
talons, clawed

at the sun, tore at
the sari of snow,
poured blood over
the pastures of vicunas.

Nevertheless the mountains were pretty quiet; movement
barely perceptible, except to geographers. But,
when the shadows of clouds flickered over them,

the air in one of its brighter moods, they had a way
with light, there's no denying. They turned it into music
the like of which you've never seen but only heard

as an echo among pines, sigh of the sea when the wind
has the scent of clover, or when you strain your ears
as the shadows of geese cross the moon.

He whispered a word that cannot be written
and turned to the south.

In their thick garments the colour of soil,
the farmers leaned against the wind, the blades

of mattocks rising and falling like the beaks
of carrion eaters. Though the sharp winds

had cracked their cheeks, furrowed their foreheads,
they laughed behind the backs of men who came

in big cars to inform them of their misery, teach
them how to be provident, and the language of a tribe

that worshipped ants. They talked regularly
and familiarly to their ancestors, told stories

of the time before the White Death and horses;
of the days when the sun was their father, the moon

a mother, and children danced by the shores of the lake
untroubled by the scruples of men who dressed as crows.

The high land continued with no lack
of imagination, taking little note
of what lay below on either hand.
Some forests, some peaks, hot deserts,
cold deserts hatched by trails of guanacos,
shadows of condors and thirsty bats;
it shouted and laughed, roared and gentled
its way through thickets, bogs to those peaks
of fires and giants, to rookeries of penguins
and seals, graveyard of white ships
where water and wind embraced in an icy bed.
Beyond, snow had its kingdom; and the breath
of that land was colder than death.

The frost burned his cheeks.
He turned to the east.

And somehow the perfume of orchids and mould drifted
up against the mist that floated down through the gorges
thundering with the congestion of rain. The nearest
trees were short, with green beards that dredged the wind,

but as the forest grew in confidence and the earth fell
away, they reached for the sun and the benison of clouds;
and their skins were smooth except for the writhing
of vines that were highways for beetles and made snakes

feel at home. The hunters of the forest had quiet voices,
unlike many-coloured parrots and macaws, and
the howling
monkeys. Fish were unusually arrogant despite a profusion
of alligators, which on moonlit nights lined the dark banks

of all the waters with their eyes, guided the slim
canoes about their business. Man and beast, finch
and spider, tree and fern, each had its territories;
so that it was as it had been, as it was before.

But

though as far as vultures
could make out there
swam a sea of green, even

sloths were uneasy,
subject to fits
of animation. Turtles

and long-nosed dolphins
became disorientated,
and some were diagnosed

to have anorexia.
Some of the hunters
blamed it on

missionaries who'd
crept into their lives;
who even followed them

in migrations to rivers
in the time of sun,
to the deep forest

in the time of rain.
There were rumours
of great beasts

carrying away
trees like an army
of leaf-ants,

but most remarked
on the grey
tendrils in the sky.

The rivers ran to meet like lovers, until they grew as wide
as a sea, were fed by the mountains and black storms
that swept the sky. But though the rain washed and
the lightning

cauterised the air, it never lasted. The reek of smoke
was insistent, the forest besieged with fire, spears of roads
drove into its heart, it was pocked with runways. Beyond

the fires, cities and deserts, ranches and hovels, ministries,
cemeteries, the ocean was little changed; it stretched
and stretched, rolled and rolled like a whale oblivious . . .

He stood very still on the shoulder
of the mountain; his limbs were stone.

WEATHER-WISE

I said to him you know the rain
has hardly stopped the last three days

He said in Patagonia there are shrews
that excrete perfume so divine that bees
are drawn from natural flowers to the shrew's
sable tongue for it to steal the golden harvest

I said maybe it will clear up this afternoon

He said in Kuala Lumpur some nights the frogs
achieve such pitches that their songs burst amber
jars of rice wine and fruit flies get drunk
frogs feed insatiably the lizards too

I said the greenhouse effect will melt the ice

He said that in North-East Australia crocodiles
have a special penchant for the blues and if
you play Miles Davis to the setting sun they turn
white bellies to the rising stars and greet
the tropic night with little grunts and purr

I said that in Estonia there are wolves
that gather every Candlemas to hold
a howl-in and their music causes bears
insomnia but passing caribou react
differently and dream erotica

He said I think you're right about the rain

ON THE BEACH

the child's eyes widened to the first sea;
a toe extended, flinched to the cold grasp.
He squealed and the wave retreated, he stumbled
forward and the sea wrapped him to his knees.

Later he discovered that mermaids were much rarer
than expected, and that although under the skin
woven by so much labour of the rain there were fish
with swords and magic lanterns and that the sea

was bent like a bow, there was a hard line drawn
between wheat and seaweed, and air was constantly
at war with its neighbour. Baffled by the contradictions
of surfaces he observed in water, he retreated

from the coastline and spent many years dividing
his time between climbing mountains – only to find
yet more air, though more refined – and cities
that he noticed bore a distinct similarity

to broken rock. Armed with a more sophisticated
conception of the universe from his studies
of chaffinches and newspaper columnists,
and having created a surface, the machinery

of arrogance carried him back within earshot of skuas
and blasphemous fishermen, and he was not so naive
any longer to believe all the stories of drunken
mariners and priests, most particularly those concerning

promenading on waters and maddening swine, cruising
the oceans in the hidden parts of whales and multiplying
fish. So he bought a yacht and hired a crew of misplaced
Latvians who had been shipwrecked whilst attempting

to discover why herring had deserted the Baltic during
the sixteenth century, and if this was in any way related
to the birth of Shakespeare. But his journeying was
  brought
up sharp by an unforeseen rock, and a cold hand on
  his toe.

THE DESERT

would appear to have been
around some time – this road an arrow
in its flight from then to when.
Mesquite and tumbling weed, cacti
with stubby arms, hands severed
as they raise them in surrender
to the sun. This is an open space
where time is measured by the skins
of snakes and music of a desiccated wind
that whistles on a tinny flute, twists
in dervish dance among the thorns until
sun fall and the sharp knives of night.

An eagle buccaneering in the sky;
a sand grouse dusts. The word is dry.

WEST OF THE MISSOURI

The tree was set high among rocks, tortured
and warped by winds. The horse and the dying man
were content with its leaking shade, lizards
cold-eyed the flies resting on the mare's flanks

and a sidewinder hankered for the flesh of geckos.
In that moment the clouds stopped, their shadows at one
with brown leaves of corn, dust, and the stagnant lake
being devoured by lilies. He got down from the horse;

undid the girth, slid the stained saddle from her back,
patted her neck before taking off the bridle. She stood
head bowed until he slapped her rump. She wheeled
and galloped down the hill to become lost in the tide

of bushes. And he began to sing a love song through
the blood in his throat. He thought: *these words
are the hoof prints of my passing, these the shadows
of lost birds, the sunset dreams of mariners. Fuck it.*

He lay down in the shade with the snake, the flies
and a posse of lizards.

THE TRAPPER

He came from a land
devoted to bears, addicted
to sleep when the north wind
ran through the shivering
maples, filled the night
with eyes. He seemed older

than any tree in the valley,
claimed more than a nodding
acquaintance with chipmunks.
He stank of a lifetime
among dead mammals, spent
all day whetting his Bowie

knife, each night setting the jaws
of gins and snares. According
to the oldest of Indians,
he'd come out of the east,
had a mermaid tattooed between
his shoulder blades, but no one

had the courage to ask him
even though he'd trapped so long
that snow was deep-drifted
in his whiskers, his teeth
worn down by ice. When found
more than asleep in his cabin,

the storekeeper and three sons
buried him in the meadow
where the moose came to court.
But the Indians dug him up,
that very night, laid him
open to the sky, in a secret

place among aspens and lodges
of beavers, left him staring
at Orion, at the still stars.
They threw his skinning knife,
his traps, far into the sheened
waters of a lake.

COSTALAGO

THE JUG

Henrique turned the palomino off the track by the abattoir
and rode along the shore of the silver lake, accompanied
by cicadas and the moans of bullocks. He stopped to light

a cigarette and let the horse crop the new grass before
suddenly driving spurs into his mount and charging
   the lake.
The hooves thrashed the water into foam and the
   sun played

magic with the spray. Henrique felt good; felt even better
because he was going to San Pedro to see Juan the *brujo*,
and it was today that Hernando came down from
   Buenos Aires,

from the sierra where there were wild goats and mescal
was fermented that drove even the oldest of men young,
and to have enormous erections. Hernando would fill
   the jug

for him; the big five litre jug strapped to his saddle.
And he licked his lips, thrust himself up in his stirrups,
opened his lungs to bellow out a song of appalling
   dimensions.

THE MEDECINE MEN

The shadows were still long when Henrique moored
   his horse
outside Juan's store, and, as it was too early for cockfights,
the street was deserted, even by dogs. The shop was dark

and smelled of death. The *brujo* emerged from behind
   a forest
of herbs and shrivelled parts of many departed species. He
poured a shot from a stone bottle into a mug for his guest.

They drank silently and solemnly until the shadows
    were gone
from the street and the sun stood still, started a fierce
discussion on the wondrous proportions of girls in
    Vera Cruz.

Various fishermen, pig farmers, two albinos and a redhead
drifted in and out, and old Bernaldo Duran said there
    would be
a second world war because of television. Paco the
    one-eyed

was ejected for stealing humbugs and Hernando's
    arrival was
heralded by clinking bottles, and when his mule came,
    sparkling
in the sun, the day was blessed, even priests forgiven.

RETOUR DE FORCE

Henrique rode from the village before the cockfights
    started.
He wanted to be alone now; the mountain dew of
    Buenos Aires
is famous for its powers of contemplation. So he
    didn't take

the path by the lake where the women would be
    washing, but
the track that passed the hacienda that had been burned
in the revolution, and was very haunted. Though the sun

had already been wiped out by the blue mountains,
    he unsaddled

the palomino, sat down on a tombstone and uncorked
    the jug.
Time wasn't noticeable, only the passage and backchat
    of birds

and distant dogs which hardly intruded at all into
    the world
that danced in his head to the rhythm of unheard music.
Rivers with dark banks ran through the desert, fat with fish

and full of laughter. The wind was bright with dragonflies,
the sky with rainbows, fields swarmed with quail. The light
was full of jade and humming-birds, thorns glistened

with the eyes of ice, and when the sunset washed
    the water,
black bulls and herds of deer grazed on silvered
    purple grass.
Only when the horse nudged him did he stopper the jug,

and the palomino knew the way through the dark to
    the stable.
In his street girls would be making up for a hopeless night
in the cantina. The jug was cool against his thigh.

HENRIQUE MONSECA AND THE DAWN

He was woken by Fulgor Galileo's donkey, its limp
making an uneven clatter on the rough paving.
He found it hard to remember when it had not.

The night floated back to him like a movie
made by gringos; how little Felicitas Benavides,
with her crooked nose and bleached hair, had danced

like Salome among the sticky tables and sweat
of the cantina. He reached out to make completely sure
that the jug was still there and for the comfort

of its eye. It gripped his hand by the first finger,
and pulling himself up onto an elbow, he took a swig.
It hit him where he hurt like a wild mustang, like,

like that was better. Henrique sat up on the bed
and became immediate. The mescal had shrivelled
his palate; he fevered for coffee. That was the beginning
of the day that saw the deflowering of Petunia Sanchez.

IN THE PLAZA EMILIANO ZAPATA

Julio Terramoto was even more indian than all
the other Indians of Costalago. It was argued
his appearance was not a major business asset

for the bar that he ran in the plaza, but others
asserted he drew people to his little stock
of tables with the hypnotic art of a rattlesnake.

Anyway Henrique was never one to engage in such
contentions and had netted quail with Julio under
a number of full moons, in the rich fields

of Don Floriano Pechuga, who owned the supermercado
and the Chief of Police. So Henrique had the table
of honour at the Bar Julio y Juanita, and such an accord

with the Most Indian that his drink was always served
without asking; the diurnal alternations from coffee,
to beer, tequila, to mescal being precisely anticipated.

And last night Julio had heard Henrique's horse returning
from the direction of San Pedro and knew that the mescal
bottled by Don Floriano's brother-in-law in Colima
    was out.

Henrique sipped his coffee still trying hard not to notice
the sun, but with a lazy but growing tolerance to all
the world, and in particular to the increasing activity

in the square, as Costalago became more awake. He noted
Chico Lopez had put his best saddle on his mare
  and would
be going up to Trochas to visit his friend Paco; consort

with Fausto Ortega's fragrant widow. Henrique considered
whether it would be profitable to call on Mercedes Lopez,
sell her a mat at least. But she was extremely pregnant.

NOON IN THE PLAZA EMILIANO ZAPATA

Under the porticos dismembered goats were subjected
to ordeal by fire and water; trestle tables
decorated with their parts and tortillas. The air

was roasted, broiled and impregnated with spitting
oil and the fiercest of spices. The serious drinkers
switched from beer to tequila for its reputed

ability to break down the flesh of hardy ungulates.
Hawkers of watermelons drove their barrows between
horses and fat buses, while from the loudspeaker

in the belfry Jesus Christ Superstar called out. Henrique
had already reached the decision that because he had
passed a black cat with only half a tail on his way

to the square, it would be unwise to engage in any but
the most pressing adventures. Julio saw how Henrique's
whole body relaxed on reaching this decision and poured

him another tequila. From this moment joy entered the day
despite the arrival of Henrique's cousin Bartolemeo,
who worked in the abattoir and went to Mass on
   weekdays,

came from a family renowned for prominent noses and
   obscene
practices with sheep and poultry, and it was said there had
been odd things born with beaks and cloven hooves.
   Henrique

was served a huge plateful of roasted goat and plump
   chicken
breasts by Maria Cisneros, who remembered how
   enthusiastic
Lola Fuentes had been about his love-making, except for

the night after the fiesta in Manzanillo. But he hardly
noticed her, fascinated by the sight of Chino Robles
being beaten in the privates with a cucumber by
   Corazon Paz.

INTERMEZZO

Henrique only realised late in the afternoon how excited
he had been by the frenzy of Corazon Paz with the
   cucumber.
He went home to his adobe in Calle Hidalgo to pick up
   his jug;

then up Allende, over Obregon, down Carranza, over
   the back
wall, among the doves, mangos, peaches of Corazon's
   garden.
He was disappointed that she didn't seem surprised, but

as their lips met round the jug and they became
   wholeheartedly
entangled, he was driven to the conclusion that
   Chino Robles
was an ass. Their passion was as wild as the great tornados

that tore whole villages to pieces; it occupied every corner
of her house at one stage or another. And when he sighed
it was for all the nights and afternoons that hadn't been;

in gratitude for what was now, for the hardness of her
breasts, strength of her enthusiastic thighs, pillow of hair,
for her widened and misted eyes; and for the cucumber.

BACK IN THE PLAZA EMILIANO ZAPATA

As the priest crossed the square Henrique made
a rude sign to his back, and grinned at Julio,
who assessed the glaze in his eyes and brought

an ice-cold beer. Henrique beckoned to a troupe
of *mariachis*, who gathered round the table, started
to play a series of bloodcurdling and sentimental

songs that blew him hither and thither and sloshed
beer, tequila, mescal and Corazon Paz's saliva around
in his stomach, until not only his blood was almost

entirely replaced, but the fumes rose up to his brain
and caused the plaza to dance like the earthquake
of 1968, and the population of Costalago to tremble.

The music induced much weeping and abrazos;
   Henrique swore
eternal friendship with one or three men he'd promised
to kill for an insult to a possible relation of Pancho Villa.

It was only when the young came, to circle the square
in opposite directions, the men outside the women,
   smirking
and giggling, that he became quietly morose, settled

his bill with money borrowed from Corazon Paz in a fit
of inspiration, left the plaza to its own devices. He sought
silence, his jug, and sanctuary on the Hill of the Virgin.

HENRIQUE AND THE VIRGIN

It was not a significant hill; more of a mound scarred
by the wind and sandals of those who climbed to the statue
of the Virgin, carrying flowers and many strange petitions.

She sat gazing down on Costalago, from the great shadow
of a rough-hewn cross. And when Henrique reached
   the top,
he sat and rested among dahlias and wild lilies, his back

against her knees; and when he offered her a drink
from his jug, wasn't offended by her stony indifference.
From the town below the music was faint; in the heavy air

the woodsmoke didn't float as high. Mescal trickled down
his throat and unshaven chin, into the raw pain of living,
and it drowned the sound of hours, the messengers

who delivered appointments, painted the hems of shadows
with phosphorescence, fields of corn with red-winged birds,
and he told the Mother of God one of his cleanest stories.

DOWN IN THE PLAZA EMILIANO ZAPATA

Nobody noticed the darkness that grew early
in the west, nor heard any of its roar, largely
because of the six *mariachi* bands, the loudspeakers

from the church and several jukeboxes, but took notice
of Celestino Gitano when he scrambled into the plaza
on his crutches, shouting and pointing over shoulders,

because he was the only one in the town to be converted
by the Jehovah Witnesses. When they saw the whirling
blackness, and heard its fury, some ran for their homes,

some out into fields, while some were frozen frigid
where they sat. Corazon Paz headed for open country
but stopped in awe when she looked up at the hill, saw

Henrique outlined against that part of the sky still bright.
She saw him stretch out his arms, and, as the twister
reached for him, he grew to a great shadow, and was gone.

THE WINGS OF ANGELS

Henrique was woken from a dream even Jesus of Nazareth
would have had problems forgiving, by the matriarch
and patriarch of tornados. He gulped down all he could

swallow from the jug, kissed the Virgin on each cheek,
turned to face the blackness that roared with the voices
of a thousand exiled lions, that had gathered in its skirts

the dust of several provinces, raped farms. It rushed over
the desert like a monstrous top, mouth of a tomb,
   and when
the sand scoured his cheeks Henrique bellowed like a bull,

stretched out his arms, and spat, and laughed. It took him
fiercely, tossed him like a leaf into the vortex of its heart.
And that was the day Petunia Sanchez was visited by
   an angel.

P.S. Floriano Pechuga's supermercado now has a section devoted to selling pilgrims' souvenirs, including photographs of Henrique Monseca, taken in Vera Cruz, with seven ladies of the night, retouched with wings and sparkling halos.

P.P.S. Petunia Sanchez has a fine son; married a carpenter.

THE OPTIMIST

His memory's none too hot;
can't even remember the day
he was born, not even the terror
of that emergence. He's sure
he cried – who wouldn't -
but he knows it was one
of those clear winter days,
snow flurries out of nowhere,
cold as a judge's smile, bright
as an axe, sharp as a lover's teeth.

And where the mountains tumble about
in the West, he searches for his tombstone,
looks into the eyes of a December
ringing with disconsolate bells.

THE PORTER

Today as he climbed he noticed
how worn the rock, and began
to hear the tide of feet

that had been before, even
his own. Then the hill
was not so steep, the mountain

still tall against the light
but not so dark, even in the heart
of the rock. The snow no longer

hurt his eyes. He stopped
where the track was a shade
wider, and though the ledge

was crowded to the lip,
he had no fear, smiled to that
company and for those below.

THE PEDLAR

comes limping with a bawdy song, the rain
his drummer, a whisky voice that smells
of paint, cockles and whelks, carnations,

and a throat-soothing balm rendered
from dogs' bones and spiced with myrrh.
He sings of his game leg, the pain

of scars, of buses missed and mountains
and their crowns. His pack bulges
and the lies drop out and blow

behind him like a bridal train. The rain
drums louder, he unships his load, spreads
out his wares and wiles, *The Birth*

of Rome, The Twilight Life of Wolves,
five volumes on *The Art of War*, a great deal
of holy books (some slightly charred),

a prayer wheel and the foreskin of a saint.
He's plastic ducks in pink and blue, condoms
to match; crossbows and credit cards, tickets

for *My Fair Lady* and the zoo. He whispers
his promises in children's ears, packs up
his unsold wares, limps back to Parliament.

NEWSCAST

a time of torn posters
blood on all the walls a day
most like any other day
a time
that lies like a politician
like any other

what are you doing here
in my sad room
wearing
your skins of transparent light
shoes of stricken deer
smile of a stockbroker

where are the twelve men and true
your waxen saints
dressed in excretions of spinning worms
ringing cracked bells
chanting liturgies
in the oiled voices of judges

do you bring the light of dead stars
to lighten
the chambers of my breath
burn in crusted ventricles
or is it truth quivering
like a netted lark

THE CRUISE OF THE SPY

They finished coppering
the hull, *The Spy* slid off
the land to swim, was filled
with pitch and riggers, swung

to each turn of tide and wind.
We filled her holds with brandy,
swords, muskets, knives, brass
pots and pans, calicoes

of bright colours, other things
to trade among the blacks.
Sails bent, the crew aboard,
dropped down to Gallions Reach

to take in gunpowder. On
to Gravesend, anchored, got
our river pay and weighed,
threw off the gaskets, hauled

round the yards, explored
the wind and laid her close,
felt her heel and reach
her muzzle out for Africa.

Far from the cool winds of home, roast beef
and beer, under a burning sun, foddered
on salt junk, foul water and a gill of rum
a day, we raised the coast of Guinea,
the Tooth Coast, where tusks of elephants

are plentiful. We came to anchor here,
between Cape Palmas and Cape Three Points,
and bartered for some ivory and yams. For fear
we kept close watches and called out from poop
to fo'castle; loudly to let the negroes know

we were on guard. To make our water last
the scuttle butt was headed up with a hole
to take a musket barrel with no breach, and
we'd to suck water through the mouth of death.

At Anamoboe we lay among
a fleet of traders. A crew
from Liverpool came aboard,
were much surprised to see

our Mr Cummings, chief mate,
(whose proper name was Thorsby)
it appeared was first officer
of *The Gregson*, Guineaman,

had thrown the ship's cook
into the boiling coffers;
jailed on Merseyside but
escaped to another name. Thence

down a bolder shore to Accra,
well supplied with pigs, goats,
yams, and fruits. Feasted,
coasted to Bonny Bar,

Bight of Benin; the sun
very hot in latitude 4.30 North.
Hauled out the pinnace,
rigged her, a fine boat,

stout, clinker built,
well capable of holding
a hundred black souls
or so.

Safe anchored, we unbent all sails, sent down
the topgallant masts, struck all the yards, began
to build a roof over the ship from masts and mats
against tornadoes; a barricade built across the deck,

wall pieces placed to fire on mutinous slaves. Four
rooms were made; the smaller one for Quaes, a savage lot
with filed teeth; a second for the gentler Eboes, a third
for boys, and all abaft the women. Slaves were brought

regularly by servants of King Pepple, whom we'd greased
with an old cannon, suit of blue edged with gold lace, cap
with feather plumes, and brandy – brandy we thought
    good
but for his taste not hot, did not bite his tonsils till

we stiffened it with cayenne peppers. Soon we'd two
    hundred
slaves of either sex. Poor creatures! What distress they
showed! Some thought we lived upon the sea and they
    our fare.
Some of the women fainted, some wailed, not few
    went mad.

Death crept about the ship
in many forms. The mate
who'd lost his name lost
his life to fever. Two

prime female slaves
slipped over the side;
a boat sent after but
they'd only swum a few

weak strokes before
the sharks had torn
them into pieces; no
fragment to be seen

except the water tinged
with blood. Another day
we saw the French aboard
a sister ship to climb

like monkeys up aloft;
were sent to quell
the mutiny with cutlasses
and shot, and left

more dinners for the fish.
But soon we'd fetched
our tally, had four-fifty
blacks, and sailed.

Now as we rolled across an empty sea
like a great tub of pickled meat,
the Captain hoisted the true colours
of his fear; curled up his lips, shot

venom from his eyes, his knuckles white
on the handle of the cat. He flogged
a female captive to the bone for stealing
cutlery; just as he'd beat a poor seaman

to his death in Anamoboe, for the losing
of an oar. Water was short, the slaves
piteous in their cries. We drove a stench
before and left a trail of flesh astern.

For all the fresh winds
of the trades swept
through the rigging,
for all the spray, all
the flying fish,
dolphins, and the stars
brighter, closer, for
all the swabbing of the decks,
the airs were heavy
with the rasp of chains,
strange songs
and hatred in the hold.

We'd poor reckoning
by the log, nearly
ran onto St Thomas
in the dark; hauled off

but never after trusted
our landfall and were much
relieved to raise Barbados,
anchor in Carlisle Bay.

On to Jamaica with a merry wind.
Moored in Montego Bay to sell
our freight, and they, though glad
to wipe their feet in dust, turned
their heads often back as they
were led away.

Note. *The real author of this poem was William
Richardson, a seaman from South Shields, whose account
of his years at sea between 1780 and 1819 is recorded in
his own words in* A Mariner of England, *published by
Conway Maritime Press.*

CHARLIE OTTOWAY

It was about ten to eleven when I went out into the street.
The world was considerably empty except for some
exceeding light
of the kind that doesn't encourage shadows but seeps
into walls,
strokes bushes, lawns and black dustbins
with soft hands.
Yet I was thinking about Concepcion Delgado
and the Sierra de Ronda, neither of whom had
anything to do
with the hour or weather,
but inhabited sharp and shadow, steel and jet;
a time filled with saffron rice
and the voices of wine.

And she smiled.
And the hills smoked.
And Tommy Fairbrother

came out of his garden and we walked together
to the Bay Horse with such precision
that Lucky Tomlinson was just unbolting the door,
greeting us with the politeness
usually reserved
for the most despised reps.

But the beer was silky and Tommy
a man of few words.

Like that one in Lowestoft
who was so ashamed of his teeth
all his neighbours talked to him in sign language,
conversed with pencils and pads until
the day he cut off his big toe
with the fly-mo,
and everyone fled the gardens,
their ears in their hands.

Sometimes silence dies in a scream.
Sometimes the shout of a world is shattered by silence.

For two years I slept in a bunk
beside the engines on that wreck of a schooner,
with its cut down masts, working the Gulf
of Mexico or the Islands,
even through the Mouth of the Dragon,
right down to Brazil.

And I lay on the bed, night after night,
in that doss house in Maracaibo,
after the ship foundered, with the music
drumming or rain beating,
and sweat-stained sheets.
But the girls had the scent of oleanders
and walked with a knowing look.

I don't speak of this,
in the Bay Horse, or Black Bull,
or at the races. For I will not
sell these secret things, nor lend them to anyone
who might fold down the corners of the pages.

I sometimes think I shouldn't
have left Concepcion Delgado for that sulky flamenco
dancer.
It was just the way the muscles worked
under the olive skin of her back,
and the wild soul of the music
that I soon found she dropped with her skirts.
And Concepcion wouldn't have me back. But then,
if I so desire, I can lie on my bed, feel
the rippling skin under the whorls on my fingers
while the feet shout louder, her black hair
seizes the candlelight and she takes a strand in her mouth;
brings the fire of Vulcan to bed.

To hell with reality.

No post again this morning. A note
under my door from Jane Forsyth
to complain about my drains. The smell
of Lisbon seemed so relevant

to its crooked streets
and fados as desolate
as a Spitzbergen wind. No wonder
so many Portuguese were drowned
in the search for spices and left
their bones along the sea roads
to the Moluccas. No wonder
we had such an empire.

It's a funny old death,
isn't it? The way one minute
is full of taut feathers, pursued
and pursuing, the next
of defeated buffalo, the next a shining river
with a cargo of fetid dogs.

I never even thought of replacing Sheba when she died:
a faithful widower. I suppose that's to my credit.
One day I will go to the moors,
for a sprig of heather to press between
the bright pages of a book. Though
it is three years now and I've moved house,
I still smell her when I come in out of the rain
and her lead hangs in the hall.

Dolly Wentwood in the newsagent's
remarked apropos of my comments on the weather
that it was a terrible way to run a country.
You should see her house.

Other people's houses are uncomforting places; not
like ships or urinals. Other people's homes,

despite deep cushions and azaleas,
are spiked.

Further along the day a great wind came hurtling;
blowing its own trumpet and spitting
like a Wardour Street tart. It was nice in the snug
when the jukebox fell quiet; the huff and puff,
rain scratching at glass. And it's a good time

to go swinging back down where the tracks converge
in the distance; into the smoke
tight woven into a curtain with shining tasselled cords
that draw it apart, revealing whatever
will be its revelation. And while this is
going on, between sipping and not sipping,
a word will dart into your ear, a cough will cough,
and, as a leaf will change the life of a river,
they will bend the light, reshape the contours
of the backdrop of blue mountains
and a very solitary volcano.

I was looking over the sea to the peak
of Tenerife, when Claudia Urzaiz
came by wearing just enough and smiled
the way she did. And that day must have been,
because I remember her uncle was as rude
as he could be in Domingo's bar,
and maybe that was why we spent
our first night together.

Ambergris is spewed out by whales,
and the origins of even Hugo Brearley go back
to the first and loudest of relevant explosions.

If you mean what I know.

PANDORA

'Sir, can I be of help?
We have this special line in lace
your wife would slaver for, and you
would stiffen like a twig, take her
on that rug that was a bear, or on
a billiard table on the second floor.'

> *Look at his paunch*
> *and piggy eyes glittering*
> *with lascivious greed. A man*
> *of substance with a worm-*
> *like dick.*

'Perhaps this jewel-studded brooch?'

> *Its price?*
> *Two miners buried in Nambibia.*

'Your wife has a more expensive one?'

> *Why not these pearls*
> *that bent a Tamil boy for life?*

'Chanel?'

> *He thinks the scent*
> *of aftershave can mask*
> *the odour of his rotting guts;*
> *his Acapulco tan can hide*
> *his dead-white underskin.*

'I'm here to please. That clock
is warranted to last, precisely
mark each second of your days; not gain
or lose a minute of your precious nights.'

Its face as faceless
as that girl in glassware
on the mezzanine he bought
with a mink jacket
at sale price.

'Look at this diamantéd sheath
that wraps my lines. How
deep the cleft; how smooth the skin;
soft indent of the thighs.'

That turns him on, the horny
and rapacious goat; makes him
break out in acrid sweat,
strut like a moorcock, reach
for his string of credit cards.

'In this department all
your desires are stocked.
This lacquered box, the lid inlaid
with golden whorls, is empty
but for a silver key.'

What would he give to take
this home? His wife? His yacht?
His shrivelled soul? This
merchandise, my billy boy,
is here to tantalise, not for
a grope.

SHIT CREEK

A mouthful of pebbles,	*A sinkful of socks,*
streets filling with eager stones,	*a house full of suds,*
air with stale semen, gutters	*running over with grease*
with sour wine	*and stale beer,*
and the incontinence	*piss stains*
of spoiled children.	*in underwear.*
I would have gone home	*I would have gone anywhere*
but for the proud-backed hyenas,	*but for the tigers*
the lice,	*hiding in doorways,*
a table of cold pies,	*hungry flies;*
smoked fish. I would	*have run away*
have taken ship, laden	*with a chest full of galaxies,*
with computers and bones,	*white gloves and frilly knickers,*
bound for Valparaiso	*in a cattle boat,*
or the islands of clashing rocks,	*to the edge of the world, but*
but for her thighs, but	*for the down on his cheeks,*
for her python lips,	*his rough chin,*
insistent ovaries.	*hard thrust.*
Just like I said,	*As I was saying,*
a mouthful of pebbles.	*a sinkful of socks.*

A TIGHT SHIP

Seamen distrust a wooden ship
that doesn't leak, has
no accommodation with the shift
of sea, and wind/wave, never weeps
or stretches to the thrust, groans
with delight or agony.

What seem the outlines
of a hard horizon are just
as ephemeral as fire fingering
the rigging in a storm,
or the bright promise
of the wake.

A tight ship is brittle
as the lives of saints, the sails
are shrouds for those
who cannot sin.

THE LOG OF THE SLOOP EXCEED

Sloop EXCEED. Nassau towards Hamilton.
Weighed anchor 2300 hrs. Wind light ENE.
Sea calm with easterly swell.

riding
the dark tide
out of moon shadow
palm shadow
out from the thrust
of music
light
love-laughter
rising
to the long rhythm
laying
a finger
on the Pole Star's eye
breathing
the body scent
of time
stealing
beyond the walls
into
the history of stone
into
the labour of Eve

EXCEED. Nassau towards Hamilton.
Hole-in-the-Wall light bearing due West.

day clean
the lighthouse
blinded
by sun that boils
pitch that seals
carapace

adrift
no bloody wind at all
we roll
and roll and drift
and roll
the great boom
crashing across
an iron sky
hull wallowing
in wash and suck
of brine
dead in the water
dead to this ocean
motionless
log line plummets
into deep blue
killers eating
predators voiceless
carnage
shadowed by wheeling
frigate birds
that mock
fallow wings

One day out of Nassau towards Hamilton.
2200 hrs. Wind light easterly. Sea calm.

night
in silver sheen
soft whispering
between hard covers
sea-night-sky-moon
fire of burning wake
language
of sight sound smell
redolence of tar
salt-touch

wind-sough
creakings
and squeal of blocks
rush of wings
voices
of wood and water
in an ancient tongue
that speaks
from mountain tops
and fens
to the silver night
and the great ocean
singing

Two days out of Nassau towards Hamilton.
Wind NNE, fresh.

luff up
helm alee
lay her down hard
on the other tack
lay the grinding coral teeth
astern
sink the land deep
drive a wedge
of pine canvas hemp and iron
into the blue plains
into the pastures
of the manatee
range of swordfish
roost of albatross
where the great wheel
of sun
and stars
has no impediment
and the wind blows true
out of the gates
of morning

Three days out of Nassau towards Hamilton.
Wind fresh, easterly.

last land buried
in the wake
the bird
a-wing scuppers
awash
cutwater slicing the peel
off soft fruit
out of soundings
there are mountains
here
    silent
all hidden in the muffled
shout and weight
of water towering
volcanos giant
squid crushed
vessels skeletons
of fish
and fishermen
no whistling
in these canyons only
songs of whales
and where they breach
we drive spray back
against a braggart wind
close-hauled and clawing
northwards
for the Bermudas

Four days out of Nassau towards Hamilton.
Glass low and still falling . . .

there's a devil somewhere
back of this wind

and the blood in the sky
and the curl of the long sea
wraps fear tight
round the belly
and the waiting
waiting
for the devil
back of this wind
this sky

Five days out of Nassau towards Hamilton.
Wind force twelve, hurricane.
Lying ahull . . .

under bare poles
the boat leaps
staggers
to the whip-
crack of this terror
that is not
wind water sky sound
but all these furies
wound about
the storm's eye
sweeping
through space
over a stripped corpse
plunging
in the race
wind/wall
water/smoke
green avalanche
a hand
has braked
the spinning
world its elements
flying

infinity
we have no hand
in this
no hope only madness
fear
breaks wild
laughter spills
into the shrieking
into the roaring
of a universe

strained timbers
shudder
to *that* anguish
this unbelief

Six days out of Nassau towards Hamilton.
Wind light southerly. Sea moderating.

water is back
to water
sky to sky
deep blue
has found
its coolness
sacred light
a sullen sea slides
under wrack under
a petrel's wing
washes over
an old grown turtle
in new found sun
Abram leans against
the mast
George squats
at the helm the sloop
lifts anxiously

towards what lies beyond
the hard line
towards long journeying
until we search darkness
for the lighthouse loom
welcome
warning
and all those other lights
fixed in memory along
the wayfaring
snakes' eyes
where the humming bird
sucks sweetness ravens
nest

don't let her broach George
sail her wing and wing
follow
the dark fin
of the albacore

FOR NEFTALI RICARDO REYES BASOALTO

'one day, rainier than other days,
the railwayman, Jose del Carmen Reyes,
climbed aboard the train of death, and so far has not
  come back.'

And when you boarded your train, Pablo,
with a steady step,
and your flag and lamp,
the roots of cedars groaned
it's said, and a great golden fish
nosed at the patient rocks
of Isla Negra.

You left a stillness
full of definite birds;
steered with the backbone of a whale
down the tired river where
willows and a bloodied cross
cast shade, sunlight was shattered
by electric screams.

Your fingers reached out
from great hams of fists
to work on wire, unwind the chains,
unyoke the stubborn oxen
from the plough.

Your flag reflected
in the waters of Jarama;
your swinging lamp the flame
of endless departures.

LAST WILL AND TESTAMENT
in memory of Anna Fissler

I leave you my breath, cantankerous
bones, various organs; to sleep
in the shade of willows, in a warm bed
among ships.

I bequeath a blunt knife, threads
of unravelled string, nets, pointed
stakes, untended acres, the scent
of almonds.

I adjure you not to forget the picnic
basket, and when you come to me with full arms,
bring a sprig of thyme, a bell full of grapes,
a gentle horse.